SUMMER IS FUN!

by Walt K. Moon

BUMBA BOOKS™

LERNER PUBLICATIONS ◆ MINNEAPOLIS

Note to Educators:

Throughout this book, you'll find critical thinking questions. These can be used to engage young readers in thinking critically about the topic and in using the text and photos to do so.

Lerner Publications Company
A division of Lerner Publishing Group, Inc.
241 First Avenue North
Minneapolis, MN 55401 USA

For reading levels and more information, look up this title at www.lernerbooks.com.

Library of Congress Cataloging-in-Publication Data

Names: Moon, Walt K., author.
Title: Summer is fun! / by Walt K. Moon.
Description: Minneapolis : Lerner Publications, [2017] | Series: Bumba books—Season fun | Audience: Ages 4–8.
   | Audience: K to grade 3. | Includes bibliographical references and index.
Identifiers: LCCN 2016001048 (print) | LCCN 2016001476 (ebook) | ISBN 9781512414127 (lb : alk. paper) |
   ISBN 9781512415339 (pb : alk. paper) | ISBN 9781512415346 (eb pdf)
Subjects: LCSH: Summer—Juvenile literature. | Seasons—Juvenile literature.
Classification: LCC QB637.6 .M66 2017 (print) | LCC QB637.6 (ebook) | DDC 508.2—dc23

LC record available at http://lccn.loc.gov/2016001048

Manufactured in the United States of America
1 – VP – 7/15/16

LERNER
SOURCE

Expand learning beyond the printed book. Download free, complementary educational resources for this book from our website, www.lerneresource.com.

Table of Contents

Summer Season

Each year has four

seasons.

Summer is one season.

The weather gets hot.

Summer comes after the

cooler spring.

The sun shines bright.

People find shade.

Why do people find shade in summer?

Summer brings storms.

Lightning flashes.

Wind blows.

Rain falls hard.

Sunlight helps plants grow.

Flowers grow.

They face the sun.

Why do flowers face the sun?

Farmers' crops grow in summer.

Corn grows tall.

It gets as tall as a person!

Animals keep cool.

They shed their fur.

Some animals are active later

in the day.

The air is cooler then.

Why do animals shed their fur in summer?

15

fireworks

16

Summer holidays are fun.

Americans celebrate

Independence Day.

Canadians celebrate

Canada Day.

Kids leave school.

They have summer vacation.

They play outside.

Some kids have picnics

in summer.

Others go to the beach

to swim and stay cool.

What do you do in

summer?

Seasons Cycle

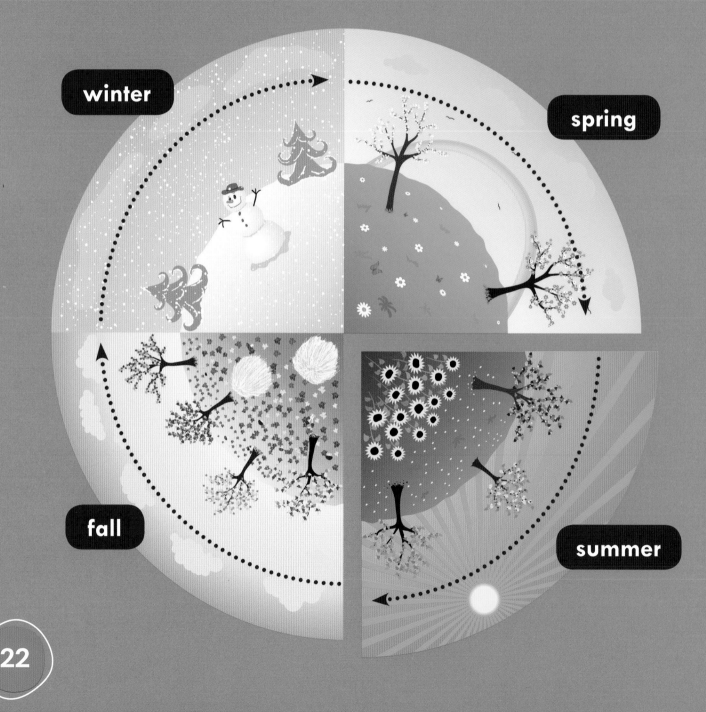

winter

spring

fall

summer

Picture Glossary

crops

plants grown for food or goods

lightning

electricity that flashes during a thunderstorm

picnics

meals that are eaten outside

shed

to lose or get rid of

Index

Read More

Anderson, Sheila. *Are You Ready for Summer?* Minneapolis: Lerner Publications, 2010.

Appleby, Alex. *What Happens in Summer?* New York: Gareth Stevens Publishing, 2014.

Herrington, Lisa M. *How Do You Know It's Summer?* New York: Scholastic Children's Press, 2014.

Photo Credits